Highlights of the 50's & 60's

50's

1951
1952
1953 1954 1955
1956 1955
1958 1957
1959

& 60's

Exclusive Distributor:
CREATIVE CONCEPTS PUBLISHING CORP.
2290 Eastman Avenue #110
Ventura, CA 93003

Catalog No. 07-1095
ISBN #1-56922-030-1

CONTENTS

CONTENTS

The Beach Boys

Herman's Hermits

The Four Season's

The Dave Clark Five

The Kinks

Elvis Presley

Eddie Cochran

Ricky Nelson

Neil Diamond

Dion and the Belmonts

The Ventures

The Penguins

Joey Dee and the Starlighters

The Olmpics

Dee Clark

Johnny Rivers

Frankie Ford

on Pickett

Lloyd Price

Dodie Stevens

Etta James

LaVern Baker

Connie Francis

Little Richard

Gene Pitney

Chubby Checker

Frankie Avalon

Rod Stewart

Mickey and Sylvia

Don and Juan

Frank and Nancy Sinatra

Bobby Day

Huey "Piano" Smith

Johnny Otis

Ray Peterson

Jody Reynolds

Isley Brothers

Brook Benton

Jerry Lee Lewis

the Songs

All Day And All Of The Night

Words and Music by Ray Davies

The on - ly time I feel al - right ___ is by your ___ side ___ ___ Girl I want to be with you ___ all of the ___ time all day and all of the night ___

Alley Cat (Song)

Lyric by Jack Harlen
Music by Frank Bjorn

Moderately Slow

He goes on the prowl each night like an Al - ley Cat,

Look-in' for some new de - light like an Al - ley Cat.

She can't trust him out of sight, there's no doubt of that.
He don't know what "faith-ful" means, there's no doubt of that.

Backfield In Motion

Words and Music by M. McPherson and M. Harden

With a triplet feel

Chorus

1. Back - field___ in
2. Off - side___ and

mo - tion, yeah, I'm gon - na have to pen - al - ize you, you.___
hold - in', yeah, you ought - a be a-shamed of your - self, ba - by.

Back - field___ in mo - tion, ba - by, you know that's a-gainst the rules.___
Off - side___ and hold - in', yeah, ___ Hold-in' on to some - one else.

fourth time repeat Chorus

out, and I caught you with... _____ First down:

belt, and I caught you with your

you start cheat-in' on me. Sec - ond down _____ I was too blind to

see. Third down: you know I love _____ you so. Fourth down:

ba - by, I got to let you go, cuz I caught you with your

to Chorus

Baby (You've Got What It Takes)

Words and Music by Clyde Otis and Murray Stein

Barbara Ann

Words and Music by Fred Fassert

Barefootin'

Words and Music by Robert Parker

Blue Rock

(1) Ev - 'ry - bod - y get off _____ your feet, You make me ner - vous when you
(2) Went to a par - ty the oth - er night. Long Tall Sal - ly was
(3) Hey lil' girl with the red _____ dress on, I bet you can bare - foot
(4) Lil' John Hen - ry he said _____ to Sue, "If I were bare - foot, would you

in your seat. _____ Take off your shoes and pat _____ your feet.
out of sight. _____ Threw 'way her wig, and sneak - ers too.
all night long. _____ Take off your shoes and throw _____ them 'way.
bare - foot too?" _____ Sue told John, "I'm thir - ty two,

Breathless

Words and Music by Otis Blackwell

Now, come on, ba - by, don't be shy, 'cause love was meant for

you and I.___ Wind, rain, sleet or snow, I will be wher -

ev - er you go. You leave me (breath out..........)

(whisper) Breath-less! Now,

Dance With Me Henry (The Wallflower)

Words and Music by Etta James and P. Otis

Cut Across Shorty

Words and Music by Wayne P. Walker and Marijohn Wilkin

But Short - y was - n't wor - ried. There was a

smile up - on his face 'cause old Lu - cy had fixed the race.

Do You Want To Dance?

Words and Music by Robert Freeman

44

Don't Break The Heart That Loves You

Words and Music by Benny Davis and Ted Murray

Don't Break The Heart That Loves You, Han - dle it with care, Don't break the heart that needs you, Dar - ling, please be

Earth Angel

Words and Music by Dootsie Williams, Gaynell Hodge and Jesse Belvin

Eddie My Love

Words and Music by Aaron Collins, Maxwell Davis and Sam Ling

54

Endless Sleep

Words and Music by Jody Reynolds and Dolores Nance

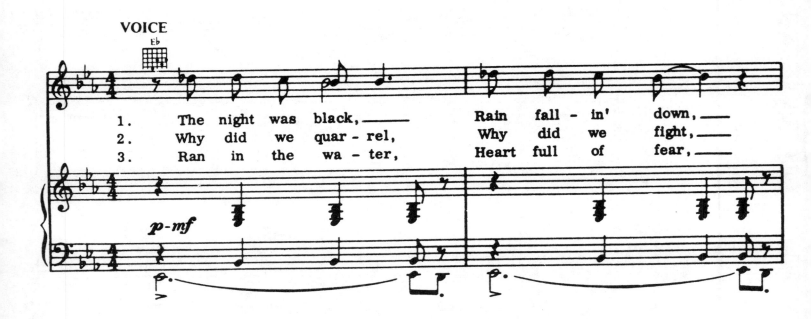

I heard a voice cry - in'___ in the deep;
My heart cried out, "She's mine___ to ___ keep,"

"Come join me, ba - by in my END - LESS SLEEP."___
I saved my ba by from an END - LESS SLEEP."___

END - LESS SLEEP.

END-LESS SLEEP, END-LESS SLEEP, END-LESS SLEEP, END-LESS SLEEP,

Hey Little Girl (In The High School Sweater)

Words and Music by Otis Blackwell and Bobby Stevenson

Goodnight My Love, Pleasant Dreams

Words and Music by George Motola and John Marascalco

High School Confidential

Words and Music by Jerry Lee Lewis and Ron Hargrave

68

Hully Gully

Words and Music by Smith and Goldsmith

Moderate Blues Rock

I Go To Pieces

Words and Music by Del Shannon

I'm Gonna Get Married

Words and Music by Lloyd Price and Harold Logan

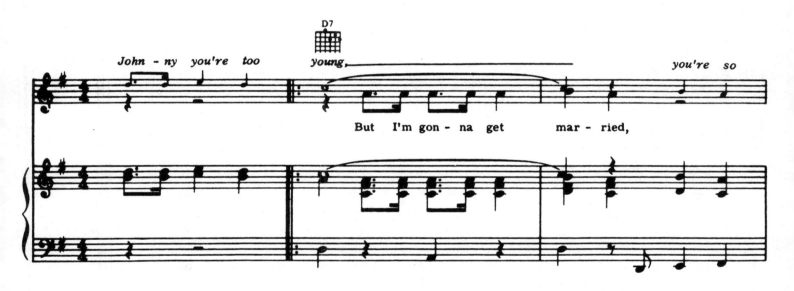

I'm Henry The Eight, I Am

Words and Music by R.P. Weston and Fred Murray

With gusto

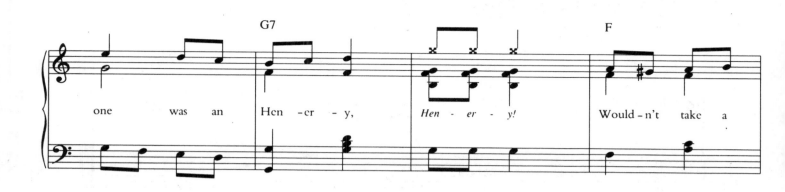

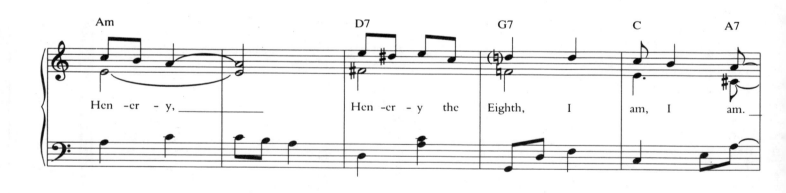

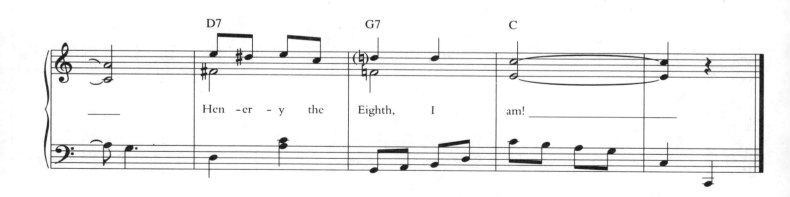

I'm Your Puppet

Words and Music by Dan Penn and Lindon Oldham

I Wonder Why

Words and Music by Melvin Anderson and Ricardo Weeks

Jim Dandy
Words and Music by Lincoln Chase

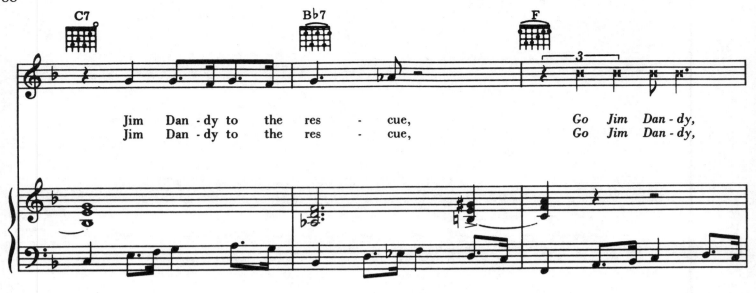

3. Jim Dandy in a submarine
   Got a message from a mermaid queen
   She was hangin' from a fishin' line
   Jim Dandy didn't waste no time.

   Jim Dandy to the rescue
   Go Jim Dandy, Go Jim Dandy.

4. Jim Dandy wanted to go to Maine
   Got a ticket on a D. C. plane
   Jim Dandy didn't need no suit
   He was hip and ready to boot.

   Repeat Chorus and Fade

Kind Of A Drag

Words and Music by James Holvay

Let's Twist Again

Words Kal Mann
Music by Dave Appell and Kal Mann

Moderately

Let's twist a - gain, __ like we did last sum - mer. _____

Yeah, let's twist a - gain, __ like we did last year. _____

Don't - cha re - mem-ber when things were real - ly hum - min'? ____

Yeah, let's twist a - gain, _ twist-in' time is here. __

Little Bitty Pretty One

Words and Music by Robert Byrd

Lonesome Town

Words and Music by Baker Knight

There's a place where lov-ers go— to cry their trou-bles a-way, And they call it LONE-SOME TOWN Where the brok-en hearts stay. You can buy a dream or two— to last you all through the years. And the on-ly price you pay

Loop De Loop

Words and Music by Teddy Vann

Love Is Strange

Words and Music by Mickey Baker and Ethel Smith

Mustang Sally

Words and Music by Bonny Rice

ride a-round Sal-ly. Ride, Sal-ly ride. ___ One of these ear-ly morn-ings,

Oh, you gon-na be wip-ing your weep-ing eyes. _____ I

bought you a brand new mus-tang 'bout nine-teen six-ty six. ___

D. S. al Fine

Now you come a-round sig-ni-fy-ing a wo-man, you don't wan-na let me ride. ___ MUS-TANG

Mary Lou

Words and Music by Obie "Young" Jessie

Out Of Limits

By Michael Z. Gordon

The Mountain's High

Words and Music by Dick St. John

Over And Over

Words and Music by Robert Byrd

Bright Rock Tempo

1. Well, I went to a dance the oth-er night,_____
2. all at once it hap-pened,_____ Well, the
3. said that she was sor-ry,_____ That
4. my poor heart was bro-ken,_____ All my

Ev-'ry-bod-y went stag, I said
pret-ti-est in this world, "Please
I was a lit-tle bit late, She would
life where had she been? But I'll

(You've Got) Personality

Words and Music by Lloyd Price and Harold Logan

Poor Little Fool

Words and Music by Sharon Sheeley

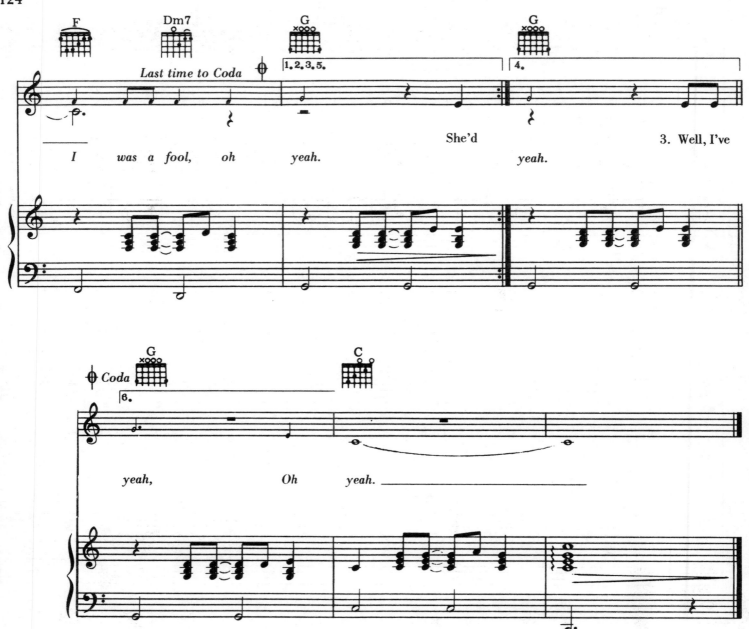

2. She told me how she cared for me and that we'd never part,
   And so, for the very first time, I gave away my heart
   Poor Little Fool, Oh yeah,
   I was a fool, Uh-huh.

3. Well, I've played this game with other hearts, But I never thought I'd see
   The day when someone else would play Love's foolish game with me,
   Poor Little Fool, Oh yeah,
   I was a fool, Uh-huh.

Rockin' Pneumonia And The Boogie Woogie Flu

Words and Music by John Vincent and Huey P. Smith

Pink Shoe Laces

Words and Music by Mickie Grant

Moderate Rock and Roll

VERSE: Spoken

1. Now I've got a guy and his name is Dool - ey He's my guy and I love him tru - ly. He's not good look - in'
2. He takes me deep sea fish-in' in a sub - ma - rine, We go to drive in mov-ies in a lim - ou - sine. He's got a whirl - y bird-y an' a
3. Now Dool-ey had a feel-in' we were go-in' to war, So he went out an' en-list-ed in a fight - ing corps. But he land-ed in the brig for
4. Now one day Dool - ey start - ed feel - in' sick, And he de- cid-ed that he bet-ter make his will out quick. He said just be-fore the an-gels come to

heav - en knows, But I'm wild a - bout his cra - zy clothes.
twelve foot yacht, Ah, but that is - n't all he's got.
rais - in' such a storm, When they tried to put him in a un - i - form.
car - ry me, I want it down in writ-ing how to bur - y me.

Rag Doll

Words and Music by Bob Crewe and Bob Gaudio

Rockin' Robin

Words and Music by J. Thomas

Sea Cruise

Words and Music by Huey Smith and John Vincent

1. Old man rhy-thm is _____ in my shoes, _____ It's no use sit-tin' and_____
2. got to get to rock-in' get my hat off the rack, _____ You know the boog-ie woog-ie hit me
3. got to get to mov-in', ba-by, I ain't liein', _____ My heart's beat-in' rhy-thm and it's

sing-in' the blues, _____ So be my guest _____ you got noth-in' to lose, _____   ⎫
right in the back, _____ So be my guest _____ you got noth-in' to lose, _____   ⎬ Won't_
right on _____ time, _____ Now be my guest _____ you got noth-in' to lose, _____ ⎭

Shout

Words and Music by O'Kelly Isley, Ronald Isley and Rudoph Isley

Surfin' Safari

Words and Music by Brian Wilson and Mike Love

Bright rock beat

Let's go surf-in' now, ev-'ry-bod-y's learn-in' how, come on a sa-fa-ri with me.

Ear-ly in the morn-in' we'll be start-in' out, __ some
ang-lin' in La-gu-na and Cerro A-zul, __ they're

hon-eys will be com-in' a-long. __ We're load-in' up our wood-y with the
kick-in' out in Do-hi-ni too. __ I tell you surf-ins run-nin' wild, it's get-tin'

Slippin' And Slidin'

Words and Music by Penniman, Bocage, Collins and Smith

Moderately (♪♪ played as ♪³♪)

Slip-pin' and a-slid-in', peep-in' and a-hid-in', been told a long time a-
Oh, __ big con-niv-er, noth-in' but a jiv-er, done got __ hip to your
Oh, __ Ma-lin-da, she's a sol-id send-er, you know you bet-ter sur-
Slip-pin' and a-slid-in', peep-in' and a-hid-in', been told a long time a-

So Fine

Words and Music by Johnny Otis

Moderately, with a beat

1. 3. SO FINE ___
(2. She thrills) me ___
SO FINE ___
She thrills me ___
SO
She thrills

FINE, yeah! ___ My ba - by's so dog - gone fine ___ She
me, yeah! ___ My ba - by thrills me all the time ___ She

(1) loves me, come rain, come shine ___ Oh ___ oh ___ yeah ___ SO
(2,3) sends those chills up and down my spine ___ Oh ___ oh ___ yeah ___ SO

Somethin' Stupid

Words and Music by C. Carson Parks

Stagger Lee

Words and Music by Lloyd Price and Harold Logan

Bright Rock

1. I was stand-ing on the cor-ner when I
2.–7. *See additional lyrics*

heard my bull-dog bark. He was bark-ing at the two men who were

gam-bling in the dark. 2. It was

153

Additional Lyrics

2. It was Stagger Lee and Billy,
   Two men who gamble late.
   Stagger Lee threw seven,
   Billy swore that he threw eight.

3. Stagger Lee told Billy,
   "I can't let you go with that.
   You have won all my money
   And my brand-new Stetson hat."

4. Stagger Lee went home
   And he pulled his forty-four.
   Said, "I'm going to the barroom
   Just to pay that debt I owe."

5. Stagger Lee went to the barroom,
   And he stood across the barroom door.
   Said, "Now nobody move,"
   And he pulled his forty-four.

6. "Stagger Lee," cried Billy,
   "Oh, please don't take my life.
   I got three little children
   And a very sickly wife."

7. Stagger Lee shot Billy,
   Oh, he shot that poor boy bad,
   Till that bullet came through Billy,
   And it broke the bartender's glass, *etc.*

Sugar Shack

Words and Music by Keith McCormack and Faye Voss

Tell Laura I Love Her

Words and Music by Ben Raleigh and Jeff Barry

Lau - ra and Tom - my were lov - ers, He want - ed to give her ev - 'ry - thing;___ Flow - ers, pres - ents and most of all,___ a wed - ding ring!___ He saw a sign for a stock car race,___

Tequila

by Chuck Rio

Too Much

Words and Music by Lee Rosenberg and Bernard Weinman

Town Without Pity

Lyric by Ned Washington
Music by Dimitri Tiomkin

Until It's Time For You To Go

Words and Music by Buffy Sainte-Marie

171

Walk Don't Run

by Johnny Smith

What's Your Name?

Words and Music by Claude Johnson

Whole Lotta Shakin' Goin' On

Words and Music by Sunny David and David Williams

- by, We got the bull by the

horn, Ev - 'ry - thing is tak - in',

Whole lot - ta shak - in' goin' on.

Wooly Bully

Words and Music by Domingo Samudio

Moderately

E♭7

1. Mat - ty told Hat - ty _____
2,3. *See additional lyrics*

A - bout a thing she saw. _____

E♭7

Had two big horns _____

Bul - ly___

Additional Lyrics

2. Hatty told Matty
   Let's don't take no chance,
   Let's not be L 7
   Come and learn to dance
   Wooly bully — wooly bully —
   Wooly bully — wooly bully — wooly bully.

3 Matty told Hatty
   That's the thing to do,
   Get yo' someone really
   To pull the wool with you —
   Wooly bully — wooly bully
   Wooly bully — wooly bully — wooly bully.

Why

Words and Music by Bob Marcucci and Peter DeAngelis

Wipe Out

By The Surfaris

Brightly, with a beat

(Improvisation)

You Talk Too Much

Words and Music by Joe Jones and Reginald Hall

Willie And The Hand Jive

Words and Music by Johnny Otis